BLAST OFF

by Kris Hirschmann

BLAST OFF

by Kris Hirschmann

Design by Bill Henderson
Illustrations by Victor Davila
Photos courtesy of NASA
Additional images by iStockphoto

Copyright © 2006 Scholastic Inc.

Tangerine Press

an imprint of
■SCHOLASTIC
www.scholastic.com

Scholastic and Tangerine Press and associated logos are
trademarks of Scholastic Inc.
Published by Tangerine Press, an imprint of Scholastic Inc.,
557 Broadway; New York, NY 10012

ISBN 0-439-55092-0
10 8 6 4 2 1 3 5 7 9
Printed and bound in China

Contents

3 . . . 2 . . . 1 . . .
Blast Off!

What comes to mind when you hear the phrase "rocket science"? If you're like most people, you think of something that is very difficult. Rocket science got this reputation because it involves things that many people don't understand, such as forces, outer space, and advanced technology. Okay, so maybe it's tricky. But it's not impossible. Anyone, especially you, can understand the basics of rocketry. This book will show you how! Rocket history, science, fun facts, and much more—it's all here at your fingertips. Get ready to take one giant step toward becoming a real rocket scientist!

Your kit includes everything you need to launch your own rockets:

Base

Rocket holder

Air pump

Tube 1

Tube 2

Blunt-nose rocket with fins

Blank rocket (blunt nose, no fins)

Curved-nose rocket with fins

In This Kit

Keep the plastic tray that holds the rocket components. Use it to store your stuff between launches.

You will need extra materials for some of the experiments and activities in this book. You should be able to find everything else you need around your home. Ask an adult for help if there's anything you can't find.

PART I:

The History of Rockets

We live in the rocket age. Space probes, space stations, and space shuttles are all things that we take for granted. We tune in to satellite-powered TV stations and get our weather reports from satellite images. Newspapers can print pictures taken by orbiting telescopes, and hikers can use satellite-provided information to find their way through the woods. None of these things would be possible without rockets!

So how did we get where we are today? Although modern rocketry is a young field, the story of rockets started a long, long time ago. Turn the page to find out how it all began.

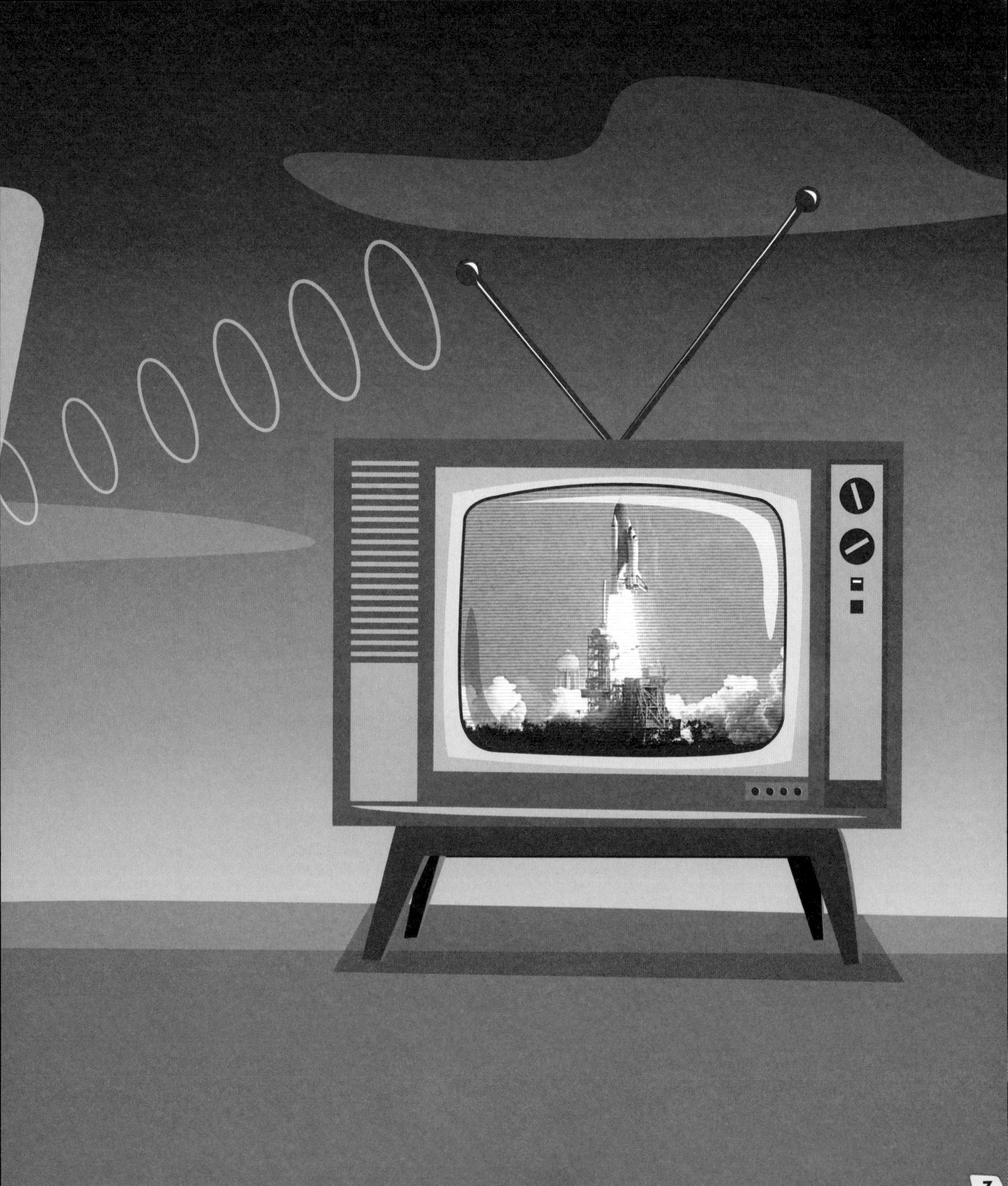

Early Rockets

The Chinese invented the first rockets about a thousand years ago. These rockets were basically tubes stuffed with gunpowder. When the gunpowder ignited, the tubes blasted into flight.

Rockets were probably first used as fireworks. But people quickly figured out how to turn these rockets into weapons. The Chinese shot their "fire arrows" at invaders. People in other parts of the world, including Europe, Arabia, and India, copied the Chinese and made rocket weapons of their own. These early weapons were small, weak, and hard to aim, so they didn't do much harm to enemy soldiers.

As the centuries passed, people tried to invent better rockets. Rocket-powered weapons did improve, but even the best rockets were still heavy, expensive, and inaccurate. By the mid-1800s, most people had given up on the idea of military rockets.

But rockets were being used in many other areas, and people began to see how useful they could be. Fireworks became popular around the world. Rocket-powered flares made good emergency signals, and life-saving rockets carried tow ropes and flotation rings to drowning sailors.

From the Earth to the Moon

Jules Verne's classic book *From the Earth to the Moon* was published in 1865. Although fiction, this book was the first realistic description of travel by rocket. Some people thought Verne's story was true, and they wrote to the author asking to be included on the next space flight!

Verne correctly applied many scientific principles in his book, but he incorrectly applied one important principle. Verne's rocket was launched from the barrel of a gigantic gun. This would never work in real life. A gunshot powerful enough to send a rocket into space would blow up the rocket and whoever was inside.

Jules Verne

FunFact

In the early 1900s, three people were working hard to advance rocket technology. Today, many consider these men to be the fathers of modern rocketry. The discoveries of Tsiolkovsky, Goddard, and Oberth paved the way for future rocket scientists.

Konstantin Tsiolkovsky of Russia

Robert Goddard of the United States

Hermann Oberth of Germany

Did You Know?

The U.S. national anthem, *The Star-Spangled Banner*, includes a line about "the rocket's red glare." Francis Scott Key wrote this line after watching an 1812 battle at Baltimore's Fort McHenry.

Rockets Go to War: The V-2

On September 8, 1944, a mysterious whistling sound was heard over London, England. The whistling was followed by a ground-shaking explosion. The explosion was caused by a German-built rocket called the **V-2**.

Built in secret, the V-2 was the most powerful rocket ever made. It could travel about 200 miles (320 km) at speeds of 3,500 miles per hour (5,630 kph). It stood roughly 47 feet (14.3 m) tall and could carry a warhead weighing more than 2,300 pounds (1,045 kg). During the last year of World War II, the German military launched several thousand V-2 rockets at targets in England, France, and Belgium.

Although the V-2 was powerful, it was not very accurate. Launching the V-2 was like tossing a ball—no one could predict exactly where it would land. Hundreds of V-2s splashed harmlessly into the English Channel after falling short of their targets. But many others made it across the channel and exploded in populated areas. Thousands of people died as a result.

The V-2 was not just the first useful war rocket. It was also the world's first space rocket! During one test, a V-2 soared 130 miles (210 km) above the earth's surface.

FunFact

HOME OF THE V-2
The V-2 was developed in Peenemünde, Germany. Today there is a museum in this city that teaches visitors about the history of this famous rocket.

V-2 rocket

VOCAB CORNER

Warhead:
Explosive cargo.

Wernher von Braun

Wernher von Braun was the scientific brain behind Germany's V-2 program. Von Braun was interested in sending rockets into space, not just in using them as weapons. At the end of World War II, von Braun convinced about 100 German rocket scientists to aid American scientists. He and his colleagues were a huge help to the U.S. space program.

Did You Know?

According to international law, there is no exact point where the atmosphere ends and space begins. But the U.S. Department of Defense states that space starts 50 miles (80 km) above the earth's surface.

Wernher von Braun

Other War Rockets

Military rockets that fall freely, like the V-2, are called ballistic missiles. After World War II, scientists began working to develop bigger and better ballistic missiles. The new rockets could travel thousands of miles before falling—all the way across continents. For this reason, they were called intercontinental ballistic missiles (ICBMs). ICBMs were no more accurate than the V-2 had been. But the purpose of these new rockets was to launch nuclear warheads. Nuclear explosions can destroy enormous areas at a time, so accuracy wasn't too important.

In later years, scientists developed guidance systems that made rockets much better at hitting their targets. Today, almost all missiles are guided.

Titan ICBM Rocket

Cruise Missile

MILITARY MISSILE TYPES
There are four main types of military missiles:
1. Ballistic missiles (true rockets)
2. Guided missiles (rockets that carry guidance systems)
3. Torpedos (underwater, propeller-driven missiles)
4. Cruise missiles (powered by air-breathing jet engines)

Torpedo

Rocket Science

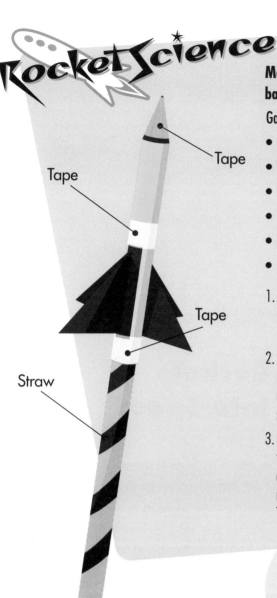

Tape

Tape

Tape

Straw

Make and launch your own ballistic missile!

Gather these materials:

- Ruler
- Scissors
- Paper
- Sharpened pencil
- Tape
- Drinking straw

1. Cut a strip of paper that measures about 1½ x 5 inches (3.8 x 12.7 cm).

2. Starting with a long side, loosely roll the strip around a pencil. Use a long piece of tape to seal the strip into the shape of a tube.

3. Line up one end of the tube with the pencil's pointed end. Make a few cuts in the tube end to make the paper easy to bend. Then squeeze the ends inward to form a cone. (The pencil point will help shape your cone.) Wrap tape around the cone to seal it. Make sure tape completely covers the cone—no air should be able to pass through.

4. Add fins to the rear of the tube. (See page 58 for suggestions.) Your rocket is finished!

5. Take the rocket off the pencil. Slide it onto a drinking straw. Blow into the straw's open end to launch your rocket.

Your straw rocket is aimed and powered at launch. After that, it travels freely. That's why it qualifies as a ballistic missile. How good is your aim? Can you see why the V-2 had so much trouble hitting its targets?

WARNING: Never aim your rocket at people or animals.

Amazing But True!

In 1958, a U.S. war plane accidentally dropped a rocket carrying an atomic bomb into the backyard of a South Carolina home. Luckily, the bomb did not explode.

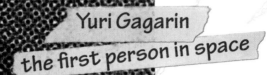

Yuri Gagarin
the first person in space

Rockets Into Space

Although war rockets were exciting, U.S. and Russian scientists had their eyes on bigger and better things. They wanted to send rockets into space, and both nations wanted to be the first to do it! In October of 1957, the Russians led the "space-race" by sending a rocket into space, launching an artificial satellite, called Sputnik 1, into Earth orbit. Less than a month later, they launched Sputnik II, which carried a dog named Laika as a passenger. Although Laika earned instant fame as the world's first space animal, she unfortunately did not survive her trip.

Sputnik

Laika

FunFact

Laika's spacecraft was nicknamed "Muttnik" by world journalists.

VOCAB CORNER

Earth orbit:
To circle the earth in space.

Artificial satellite:
Any man-made object in Earth's orbit.

Cosmonaut:
A Russian term for astronaut.

The next challenge for scientists would be to send a person into space. Who would be able to do it first? Once again, the Russians came out ahead when they launched a spacecraft called the Vostok 1 on April 12, 1961, with Cosmonaut Yuri Gagarin aboard. Gagarin circled the earth once before safely splashing down into the ocean. The incredible trip took only 108 minutes.

Big Rocket, Small Satellite

A rocket called the R-7 that weighed nearly 600,000 pounds (270,000 kg) launched the **Sputnik I** satellite, weighing only 184 pounds (84 kg), into space.

R-7 highest flight: 1,200 miles (1,930 km)

MERCURY SPACE PROGRAM

The Russians were leading the space-race, but the U.S. made an incredible comeback in May of 1961. Launching Astronaut Alan Shepard into space was the first of six manned flights of the first NASA space program called Project Mercury. A few days later, former U.S. President John F. Kennedy made a bold speech to the nation. Kennedy challenged America to put a man on the moon by the end of the decade. Could it be done? No one knew. But people were thrilled by Kennedy's vision.

Carpenter Launch

Scott Carpenter's Aurora 7 Mercury Atlas rocket lifts off from Pad 14, Cape Canaveral, Florida, on May 24, 1962.

Less than a year later, U.S. Astronaut John Glenn became the first person ever to travel into Earth orbit. Launched in February of 1962, Glenn's spacecraft, called Friendship 7, circled the planet three times before returning safely to Earth.

Although an actual moon landing had not yet been achieved, advances in technology were pointing rocketry in that direction. Project Mercury's successful flights came to an end in 1963. This made way for the next space program, Project Gemini, which was the second of the three manned space programs leading to Kennedy's ambitious dream.

Man on the Moon

NASA'S GOALS FOR PROJECT MERCURY WERE SPECIFIC:
1. To orbit a manned spacecraft around Earth
2. To test how well humans could function in space
3. To recover both spacecraft and astronauts safely

NASA:
Part of the U.S. government responsible for spaceflight and aviation. NASA is short for National Aeronautics and Space Administration.

Here is an excerpt from President Kennedy's 1961 speech.

"I believe that this nation should commit itself to achieving the goal, before this decade is out, of landing a man on the moon and returning him safely to the earth. No single space project in this period will be more impressive to mankind, or more important for the long-range exploration of space; and none will be so difficult or expensive to accomplish. ...But in a very real sense, it will not be one man going to the moon. All of us must work to put him there."

PROJECT GEMINI

Project Gemini involved 12 flights, including two unmanned flight tests of the equipment. Its two-man crew gave it the name Gemini for the third constellation of the Zodiac and its twin stars, Castor and Polluz.

Project Gemini accomplished its first and second goals – and a bridge to the moon had been built.

NASA'S GOALS WERE:
1. To subject humans and equipment to space flight for as long as two weeks at a time
2. To send and maneuver space vehicles to a docking station
3. To perfect methods of entering the atmosphere and landing at a pre-selected point on land

Ed White and Jim McDivitt

June 1965

GT-4 Prelaunch

March 1966

APOLLO SPACE PROGRAM

The final program to reach the moon was the Apollo Space Program, announced in 1968. It had been seven years since the president had asked America to put a man on the moon—and now the dream was finally within reach.

LIKE ALL OF ITS SPACE PROGRAMS, NASA HAD CLEARLY DEFINED GOALS:
1. To advance space exploration through new technology
2. To have the United States lead the space-race
3. To continue exploring the moon
4. To develop the capability for humans to work in a lunar environment

Apollo 11 Saturn V Launch

(Left to right) Astronauts Gus Grissom, Ed White, and Roger Chafee were scheduled for the original Apollo 1 mission when tragedy struck. A fire swept through their command module on the launch pad, killing all three men.

Apollo 1 through Apollo 10 were all successful missions, and each of them helped clear a path for man to get to the moon. Finally, after eight days, three hours and 18 minutes of travel-time, astronauts aboard the Apollo 11 spacecraft broadcast these words down to Earth:

"Houston, Tranquility Base here. The eagle has landed."

On July 20, 1969, Apollo 11 would triumphantly go down in history as the first spacecraft to land on the moon. The astronauts on board, Neil Armstrong, Michael Collins, and Edwin "Buzz" Aldrin, Jr., became the first men to reach the moon. Eventually, they all returned safely to Earth.

Lunar Module

SPACE SHUTTLE PROGRAM

Launching a winged spacecraft that could return to Earth and land on a runway like an airplane was just a dream back in the 1960s. In the 1970s, it became a dream come true! Officially called the Space Transportation System (STS), the space shuttle launched its first test missions in September of 1976. Since then, it has launched more than 100 successful operations and has brought space exploration to new heights.

Space Shuttle Description

The space shuttle is different from the rockets that came before it. Not only can it land on a runway like an airplane, but it also has sections that can be re-used. The space shuttle is made up of three general sections:

Reusable Orbiter Vehicle (OV)

This looks like an airplane and is where the astronauts "live."

Expendable External Tank (ET)

This part becomes separated from the space shuttle. It is not re-usable.

Two Reusable Solid Rocket Boosters (SRBs)

These powerful rockets provide the thrust to lift the space shuttle off the launch pad.

The name of the first space shuttle orbiter was changed from Constitution to Enterprise after Star Trek fans staged a campaign.

Space exploration can be very dangerous—and astronauts risk their lives when they travel into space. In a 17-year period, two space shuttle missions, Challenger in 1986 and Columbia in 2001, met with disaster. Sadly, all seven astronauts on board both of these shuttles lost their lives.

MODERN SPACE PROGRAMS

Did You Know?

Space stations are partly built in orbit! Rockets carry new pieces into space. Then astronauts put the pieces together during spacewalks, or EVAs (extravehicular activities). U.S. astronauts train for EVAs in a giant water tank called the Neutral Buoyancy Laboratory.

Space exploration has come a long way since its beginning. With the help of rockets, people today are doing things that seemed impossible just a few decades ago.

What's so amazing about today's space technology? For one thing, people can now live in space. Permanent stations like Skylab, Mir, and the International Space Station allow astronauts and cosmonauts to spend years in orbit. Long missions give scientists extra time to conduct experiments.

Equipment can also be launched into space. The Hubble Space Telescope, for example, was launched in 1990. This allows scientists to view pictures of galaxies 13 billion light years away!

Skylab

VOCAB CORNER

Light year:
The distance light travels in one year. The actual distance is about 5.88 trillion miles (9.46 trillion km).

Modern space technology also allows us to learn more about our own planet. Today, satellites monitor the earth from space. These satellites send information and pictures back to scientists, which helps them study and predict weather patterns.

Today, many nations with many different interests take part in space exploration. Some nations have programs to explore new planets, like Mars. Others are dedicated to improving life on space stations. And there are even nations working to make space travel something in which regular people could take part.

Taking advantage of Mars's closest approach to Earth in eight years, astronomers using NASA's Hubble Space Telescope have taken the space-based observatory's sharpest views yet of the Red Planet. The telescope's Wide Field and Planetary Camera 2 snapped these images between April 27 and May 6, 1999, when Mars was 54 million miles (87 million kilometers) from Earth.

act site of NASA's Mars Exploration Rover Opportunity

Famous Rockets

R-7
1957

This rocket launched Sputnik 1, the world's first artificial satellite, into orbit.

Length: 98 feet (30 m)

JUPITER
1959

A Jupiter rocket launched two monkeys named Able and Miss Baker into space. The monkeys spent 15 minutes in space before safely returning to Earth.

Length: 60 feet (18.3 m)

VOSTOK 1
1961

This modified R-7 rocket launched the first person, Cosmonaut Yuri Gagarin, into Earth orbit.

Length: 126 feet (38.4 m)

REDSTONE
1961

The Redstone rocket launched the first U.S. astronaut, Alan B. Shepard, Jr., into space.

Length: 69 feet (21 m)

ATLAS
1962

The Atlas rocket blasted Astronaut John Glenn and his Friendship 7 spacecraft into Earth orbit.

Length: 83 feet (25.3 m)

TITAN II
1965

The Titan II launched 10 manned Gemini flights between 1965 and 1966.

Length: 103 feet (31.4 m)

Famous Rockets

SATURN 1B
1968

A Saturn 1B rocket launched the Apollo VII astronauts into space. A Saturn 1B also launched three Skylab missions in 1973 and made its last flight in 1975.

Length: 167 feet (51 m)

SATURN V
1968

The Saturn V was the mightiest rocket ever built. This gigantic vehicle weighed more than 3,000 tons at takeoff, and it could produce nearly 9 million pounds of thrust. A Saturn V rocket launched Apollo 11, the mission that landed the first humans on the moon.

Length: 363 feet (110.6 m)

TITAN 3E
1974

The Titan 3E launched the Viking missions to Mars and the Voyagers to Jupiter, Saturn, and beyond.

Length: 157 feet (48 m)

ARIANE FAMILY
1979

France owns the Ariane family of rockets, which launch from a facility in French Guyana. Any nation can hire an Ariane to carry a payload into space.

Length: 177 feet (54 m)

SPACE SHUTTLE
1981

The space shuttle blasted off for the first time on April 12, 1981. By the year 2004, 113 space shuttle missions had been flown.

Length: 184 feet (56.1 m)

H-II
1994

The H-II is a Japanese commercial rocket. Ten H-II rockets launched payloads into space that were paid for by private companies.

Length: 161 feet (49 m)

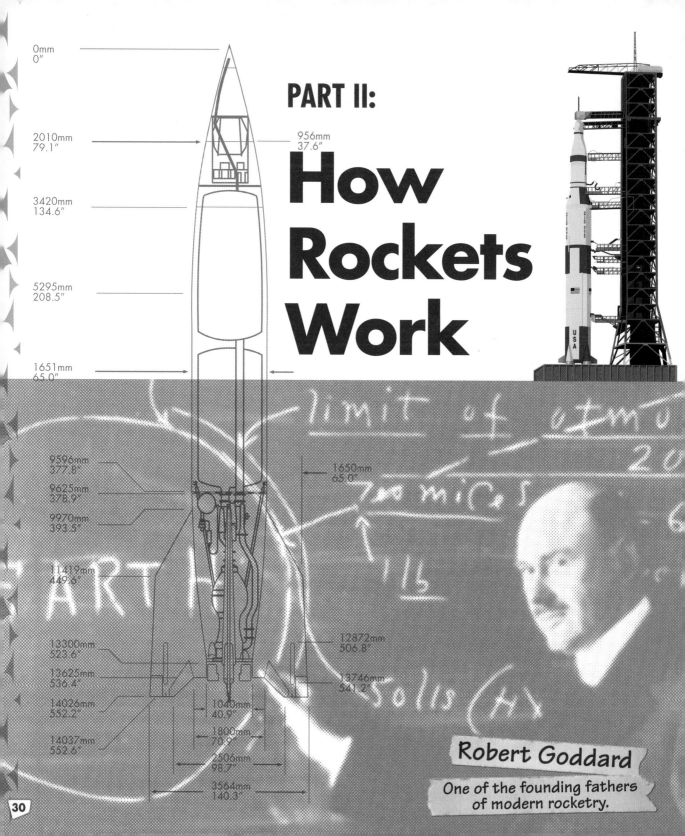

PART II

How Rockets Work

0mm
0"

2010mm
79.1"

956mm
37.6"

3420mm
134.6"

5295mm
208.5"

1651mm
65.0"

9596mm
377.8"

9625mm
378.9"

1650mm
65.0"

9970mm
393.5"

11419mm
449.6"

13300mm
523.6"

12872mm
506.8"

13625mm
536.4"

13746mm
541.2"

14026mm
552.2"

1040mm
40.9"

14037mm
552.6"

1800mm
70.9"

2506mm
98.7"

3564mm
140.3"

Robert Goddard

One of the founding fathers of modern rocketry.

At first glance, rockets look pretty simple. You just turn the engine on and they blast off, right? Wrong! Launching a rocket is complicated. Scientists have to understand many different forces and how they affect a rocket's flight. They must also consider a rocket's fuel, design, and flight path. Then they have to figure out a way to control all of these things at once. It's incredibly tricky.

Like any subject, rocketry can be broken down to the basics. This section will help you to understand a few essentials of rocket flight.

Saturn V under construction

Saturn V

Wind Tunnel testing

Newton's Third Law

In the late 1600s, an English scientist named **Isaac Newton** came up with three rules, or laws, to explain motion. Newton's third law is very important in rocketry. This law states:

For every action, there is an equal and opposite reaction.

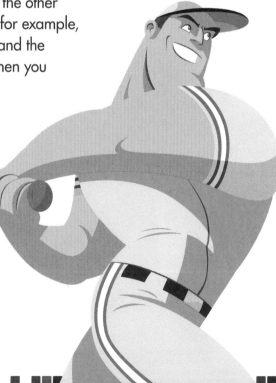

Isaac Newton

There are a couple of things to understand here. Let's start with "opposite." This basically means that when something moves in one direction, something else moves the other way. When a gun fires, for example, a bullet shoots forward and the gun jerks backward. When you hit a baseball with a bat, the ball flies forward (or up or sideways, depending on your skill!), and the bat is pushed the other way.

As you've probably noticed, however, a baseball bat does not bounce backward as much as a ball moves forward. That's where the "equal" part comes in. Things shift in proportion to their weight. A person holding a bat weighs a lot more than a baseball. So the bat and batter might move just a little bit while the baseball zips to the other end of the field. The amount of force acting on both objects is the same, but the result is very different.

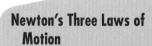

Newton's Three Laws of Motion

1. Objects at rest will stay at rest and objects in motion will stay in motion in a straight line unless acted upon by an outside force.
2. Force equals mass times acceleration.
3. For every action, there is an equal and opposite reaction.

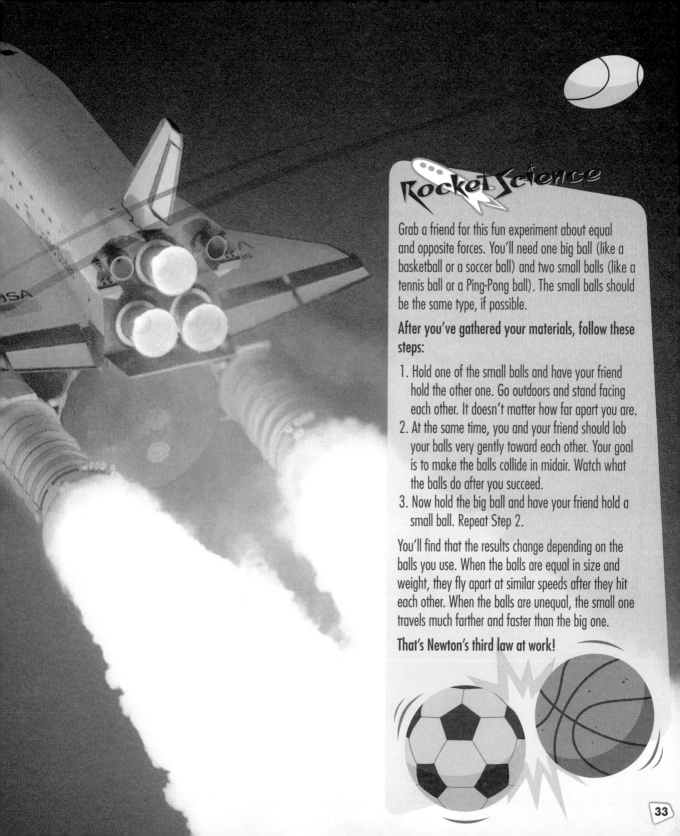

Rocket Science

Grab a friend for this fun experiment about equal and opposite forces. You'll need one big ball (like a basketball or a soccer ball) and two small balls (like a tennis ball or a Ping-Pong ball). The small balls should be the same type, if possible.

After you've gathered your materials, follow these steps:

1. Hold one of the small balls and have your friend hold the other one. Go outdoors and stand facing each other. It doesn't matter how far apart you are.
2. At the same time, you and your friend should lob your balls very gently toward each other. Your goal is to make the balls collide in midair. Watch what the balls do after you succeed.
3. Now hold the big ball and have your friend hold a small ball. Repeat Step 2.

You'll find that the results change depending on the balls you use. When the balls are equal in size and weight, they fly apart at similar speeds after they hit each other. When the balls are unequal, the small one travels much farther and faster than the big one.

That's Newton's third law at work!

Up, Up, and Away!

Now let's talk rockets! Rockets take off because of a force called thrust, which is just a way of saying how hard a rocket's engine(s) can push. Thrust is created when fuel burns, releasing gas molecules inside a rocket. The molecules bounce around vigorously. They are tiny compared to the rocket, but there are billions and billions of them. Billions of teeny pushes add up to one big shove that eventually forces the rocket off the ground.

Interestingly, the molecules that escape as exhaust are not the ones doing the pushing. It's the molecules still inside the rocket that

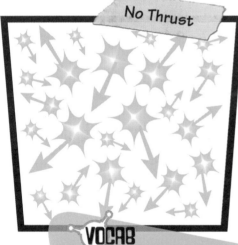

No Thrust

VOCAB CORNER

Molecule:
A group of atoms. A molecule is the smallest possible chunk of a chemical compound.

Exhaust:
The stream of molecules leaving a rocket's engine.

Thrust

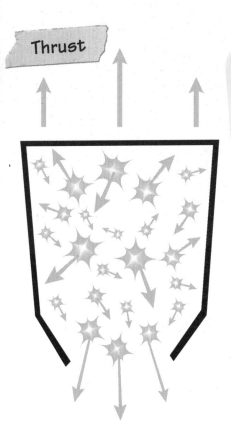

Something as simple as a balloon can show you how thrust works! Blow up a balloon and hold it closed. The balloon doesn't go anywhere because the molecules inside are bouncing equally in all directions. But if you release the balloon's stem, you give some molecules an escape route. Pressure increases on the opposite side of the balloon, shoving the object forward through the air.

Thrust vs. Weight

Thrust is usually described in pounds or kilograms. In order for a rocket to launch, its thrust must be greater than its weight. A rocket that weighs 2,000 pounds (3,218 kg), for instance, must produce more than 2,000 pounds of thrust. If it doesn't, it cannot leave the ground.

Forces at Work

Thrust is just one of four forces at work during a rocket launch. The other three are:

- Drag (air resistance)
- Gravity (the earth's pull)
- Lift (an upward push created by airflow)

do all the heavy lifting. How does it work? Look at the box above and on page 34. Both boxes are filled with bouncing dots. The first box is closed, so the dots bounce equally off all of the box's inner surfaces. The forces cancel each other out and the box doesn't move. The second box is open at the bottom, allowing some dots to escape. That means there is no pressure on the bottom of the box, but there is still a great deal of pressure at the top. The box is therefore being pushed upward. If the push is strong enough, the box will rise—just like a rocket!

Rocket Fuel

All of a rocket's power comes from its fuel. There are two types of rocket fuel: solid and liquid. Rockets are designed differently depending on the type of fuel they use.

A **solid-fuel rocket** contains a core of solid or powdered propellant. A hollow shaft runs through the propellant. This shaft acts as the rocket's combustion chamber (the place where burning happens). When the propellant ignites, exhaust builds up in the shaft and eventually shoots out of a nozzle at the rear of the rocket. Thrust is created, and the rocket launches.

VOCAB CORNER

Combustion:
The process of burning.

Propellant:
The combination of rocket fuel and oxidizer.

Reaction:
A chemical change.

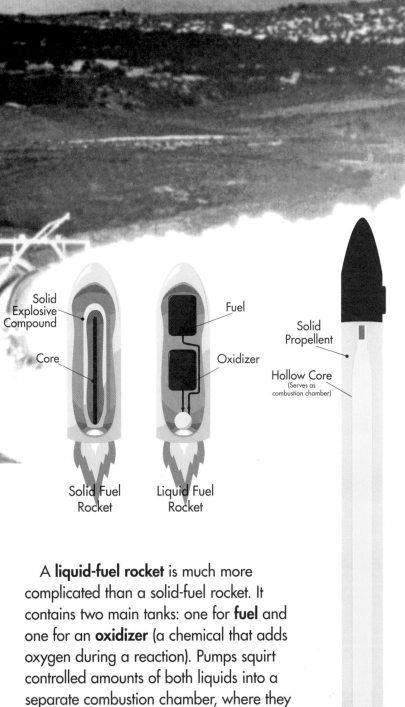

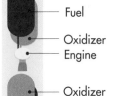

Did You Know?

Nothing can burn without oxygen—but there is no oxygen in space. So rockets have to carry their own oxygen supply. That's why liquid-fuel rockets have an oxidizer tank. In a solid-fuel rocket, the oxidizer is mixed right into the fuel.

Solid Explosive Compound

Core

Fuel

Oxidizer

Solid Fuel Rocket

Liquid Fuel Rocket

Solid Propellent

Hollow Core
(Serves as combustion chamber)

Nozzle

Fuel

Oxidizer

Engine

Oxidizer

Fuel

Oxidizer

Fuel

Engines

A **liquid-fuel rocket** is much more complicated than a solid-fuel rocket. It contains two main tanks: one for **fuel** and one for an **oxidizer** (a chemical that adds oxygen during a reaction). Pumps squirt controlled amounts of both liquids into a separate combustion chamber, where they ignite. The combustion chamber of a liquid-fueled rocket is called the engine. More fuel is pumped into the engine as needed.

Rocket Science

When a solid-fuel rocket ignites, the fuel burns until it is gone. The reaction cannot be slowed or stopped. A liquid-fuel rocket, on the other hand, can be finely controlled. Reducing the flow of the rocket's fuel and oxidizer can slow or even stop the burning process.

You can try this yourself!
To simulate solid fuel:

1. Fill a cup with water.

2. Get an indigestion tablet (like Alka-Seltzer®). Imagine that this tablet is your propellant. Drop the tablet into the water and watch as it bubbles away to nothing. Just like solid fuel, the reaction speed cannot be changed.

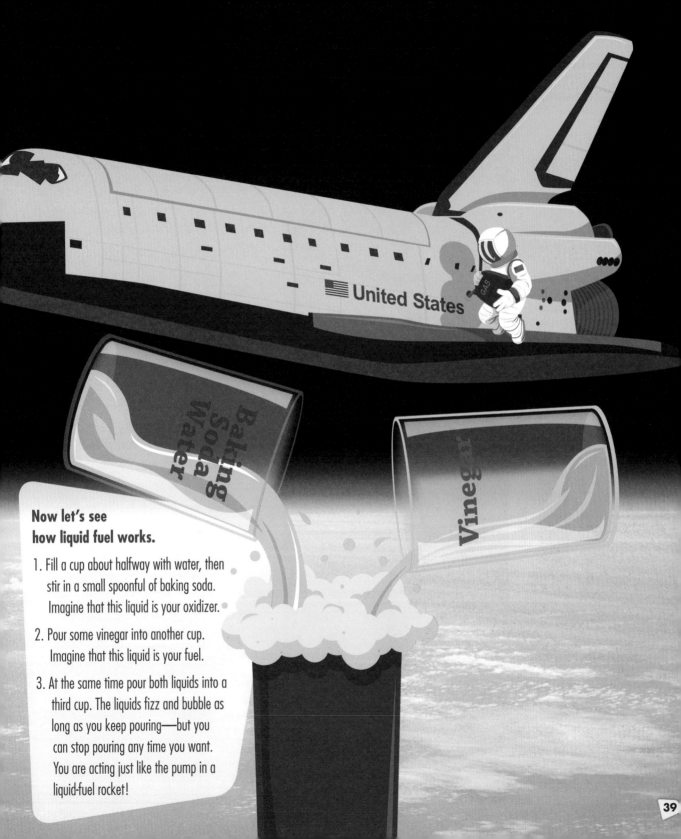

**Now let's see
how liquid fuel works.**

1. Fill a cup about halfway with water, then stir in a small spoonful of baking soda. Imagine that this liquid is your oxidizer.

2. Pour some vinegar into another cup. Imagine that this liquid is your fuel.

3. At the same time pour both liquids into a third cup. The liquids fizz and bubble as long as you keep pouring—but you can stop pouring any time you want. You are acting just like the pump in a liquid-fuel rocket!

Rocket Stages

It takes a lot of power to push a rocket all the way into space. To hold all the propellant it needs, a space rocket must be very big—and very heavy. This fact was a problem for early scientists. Was it possible to build a rocket big enough to hold the fuel it needed, yet light enough to reach space-travel speeds?

The answer is yes! It turns out that the problem can be solved by building rockets in stages. Each stage contains its own propellant source, so a multistage rocket is actually like several rockets stacked on top of each other.

Most modern rockets have two or more stages. The first stage, which is called the booster, launches the rocket. It lifts itself and all the other stages. When the booster runs out of fuel, it detaches and falls away. The next stage then ignites and pushes the rocket, which is now much lighter, even higher and faster. This process continues until only one stage is left. The last stage pushes the payload (the non-engine part of the rocket) into space. The payload is the part that performs a mission, like orbiting the earth or traveling to another planet.

RocketScience

You can use balloons and some other simple materials to make your very own multistage rocket! Here's how.

Gather these things:
- Scissors
- Styrofoam® cup
- 2 balloons (long, thin type)
- Binder clip
- Masking tape
- 2 non-bendable drinking straws
- 6½-foot (2-m) wooden dowel
  (thin enough to fit through the straws)

1. Cut the Styrofoam® cup so you have a continuous ring.
2. Inflate one balloon until it is about ¾ full. Hold the stem closed.
3. Partly inflate the other balloon. Slip the Styrofoam® ring over the balloon tip. (Look at the picture to see how this works.)
4. Pull the stem of the first balloon through the Styrofoam® ring.
5. Finish inflating the second balloon. As the balloon gets bigger, it will squeeze the stem of the first balloon shut.
6. Use a binder clip to close the second balloon's stem.
7. Use masking tape to attach the straws to the balloons. The straws must line up with each other.
8. Thread the wooden dowel through the straws.
9. Go outdoors. Push one end of the dowel into the ground, then remove the binder clip. Watch as your multistage rocket explodes into flight!

VOCAB CORNER

G-Force

Unit of force equal to the force that is created by gravity.

— Third Stage

— Second Stage

— First Stage

G-Whiz

A multistage rocket travels very slowly at first, when it is heaviest. It moves faster and faster as stages fall away and the rocket gets lighter. The acceleration process is slow enough to keep astronauts healthy. If a rocket reached its final speed too quickly, the forces involved would squash the people inside!

UNITED STATES

USA

USA

Trajectories

Rocket flights are carefully planned. Why? To perform its task, a rocket must follow a certain path, or **trajectory**. A war missile, for instance, must travel toward a specific target. A rocket that launches a satellite must reach a precise speed and height before releasing its payload. Calculating the proper trajectory is essential! If scientists make even a tiny mistake, the mission might fail.

Thanks to advanced computers, however, mistakes are very seldom made. Before liftoff, computers use complicated mathematical equations to figure out a rocket's flight path. They continually monitor the rocket's trajectory during flight. If the rocket starts to veer off course, its position can be corrected long before disaster strikes.

Computer steering is so accurate that a rocket doesn't even have to be launched at a certain angle. It can blast straight up from a launch pad. Once the rocket is in the air, computers tilt it to the proper angle to complete its mission.

What's Your Angle?
Launch angle is very important for fireworks and other rockets that can't be steered. A low launch angle causes a long, low trajectory. A higher launch angle causes a shorter, higher trajectory.

High Angle

Low Angle

VOCAB CORNER

"Trajectory" isn't just a rocket word. It also applies to golf balls, bullets, and anything else that curves through the air.

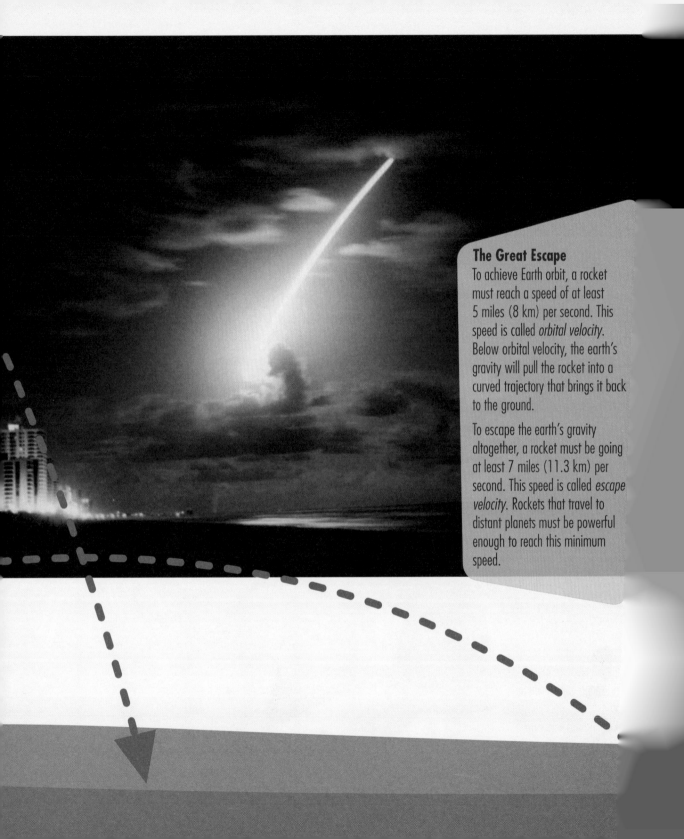

The Great Escape

To achieve Earth orbit, a rocket must reach a speed of at least 5 miles (8 km) per second. This speed is called *orbital velocity*. Below orbital velocity, the earth's gravity will pull the rocket into a curved trajectory that brings it back to the ground.

To escape the earth's gravity altogether, a rocket must be going at least 7 miles (11.3 km) per second. This speed is called *escape velocity*. Rockets that travel to distant planets must be powerful enough to reach this minimum speed.

Rocket Control

In the last section, you found out how important it is to control a rocket's trajectory. But how is this actually done?

The most basic way of controlling a rocket involves fins. Fins keep a rocket steady by "catching" air any time the rocket wobbles off course. Air pressure on the fins forces the rocket back to centered flight. Because the fins do not move, they are called *passive controls*.

Other rocket controls are active, which means they can be adjusted during flight. Some rockets have computer-controlled fins that can shift as needed. Rockets may also be able to pivot their rear nozzles to change their exhaust's direction. Doing this changes the thrust direction and the rocket's course.

Small rockets called *vernier rockets* are also used for steering. These devices are mounted on the outsides of some large rockets. They fire sideways, up, or down as needed to create a little bit of thrust. This thrust nudges a rocket back onto its correct trajectory.

RocketScience

The earth's spin makes rockets follow a curved path after launch. See how this works for yourself!

1. Tape a large target to a tree, a fence, or another outside object.

2. Position a rotating chair a short distance from the target. (Ask an adult for permission to take the chair outside.) Hold a ball and sit in the chair.
3. Have a friend spin the chair slowly. Try to toss the ball and hit the target.

Did you come close? Probably not! You'll discover that the ball does not fly in a straight line after you throw it. Because the ball is already in motion, it curves to the side in addition to traveling forward. It's hard to hit the target.

Now imagine the challenge of sending a rocket to the moon, a distant planet, or any other space object. Because the target object is moving, a rocket cannot be aimed directly at the object. It must go where the object is expected to be sometime in the future, when the rocket is due to arrive. And all this must be done from a moving start. Talk about tricky!

Did You Know?

If it takes three days to get to the moon, you need to aim your rocket where the moon will be in three days, not where it is now.

Rocket Science

People have known for centuries that spinning projectiles are more stable than those that do not spin. Some early rockets had spinning parts that kept them steady during flight.

See for yourself how spinning affects a flying object. All you need is a football and someone who knows how to throw it. Here's what you do:

1. Find an open field where you can't hurt anything or anyone.
2. Toss the football using a spiral throwing technique. See how the ball flies in a clean, steady arc?
3. Go fetch the football. Then throw it again using

a sloppy throwing technique. Just shove it out of your hands any old way. Watch the ball tumble end over end as it moves through the air.

Still not convinced that spin makes a difference? Try this experiment using a flying disc, the ultimate spinning flight toy. It's not as much like a rocket as a football is, but it uses the same principle to balance itself as it travels.

VOCAB CORNER

Projectile:
Any flying object that is put into motion by an external force.

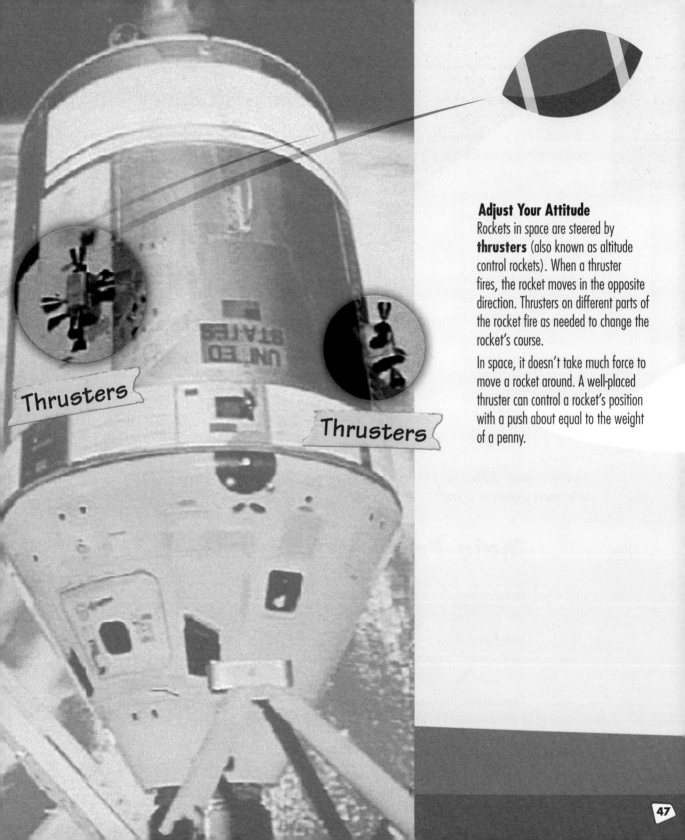

Thrusters

Thrusters

Adjust Your Attitude

Rockets in space are steered by **thrusters** (also known as altitude control rockets). When a thruster fires, the rocket moves in the opposite direction. Thrusters on different parts of the rocket fire as needed to change the rocket's course.

In space, it doesn't take much force to move a rocket around. A well-placed thruster can control a rocket's position with a push about equal to the weight of a penny.

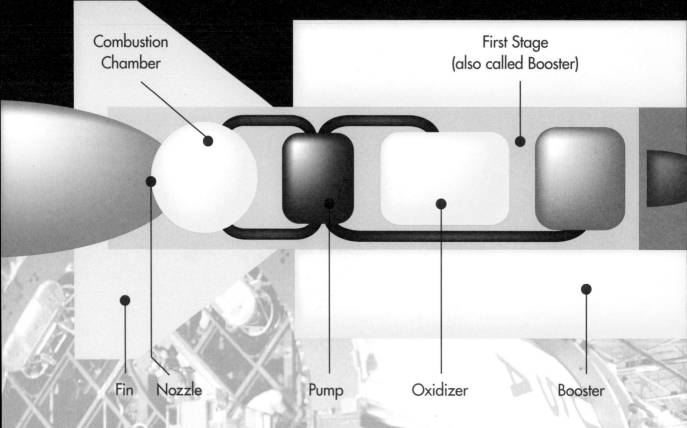

Combustion Chamber

First Stage (also called Booster)

Fin   Nozzle   Pump   Oxidizer   Booster

Main Parts of a Rocket

Body:
The rocket's core and everything it contains.

Booster:
The first stage of a rocket. Also any extra solid-fuel tanks carried by a rocket.

Combustion chamber:
A chamber inside the rocket where fuel and oxidizer are combined and ignited.

Fins:
Wings at the rear of the rocket.

Fuel and oxygen lines:
Tubes that carry fuel and oxygen from their holding tanks to the pump and combustion chamber.

Fuel tank:
A tank inside the rocket that holds fuel.

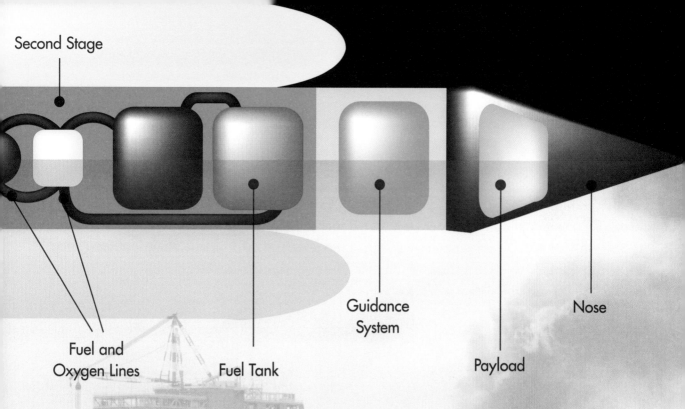

Second Stage

Fuel and
Oxygen Lines

Fuel Tank

Guidance
System

Payload

Nose

Guidance system:
Computer-controlled equipment that controls the rocket's speed, direction, and other variables.

Nose:
The tip of the rocket.

Nozzle:
An opening below the combustion chamber from which exhaust escapes.

Oxidizer tank:
A tank inside the rocket that holds oxidizer.

Payload:
Anything carried by a rocket that is not part of the propulsion system.

Pump:
Forces fuel and oxidizer into the combustion chamber at the proper rate.

Stage:
A rocket section that has its own propellant.

PART III:

Model Rockets

By this point in the book, you're probably dying to get your hands on some rockets. Of course you can't get your own space rocket, but you can launch less powerful vehicles. Anyone can buy or make model rockets. You can also launch the air rockets included with this kit. You can even conduct flight experiments like a real rocket scientist. Let's learn how!

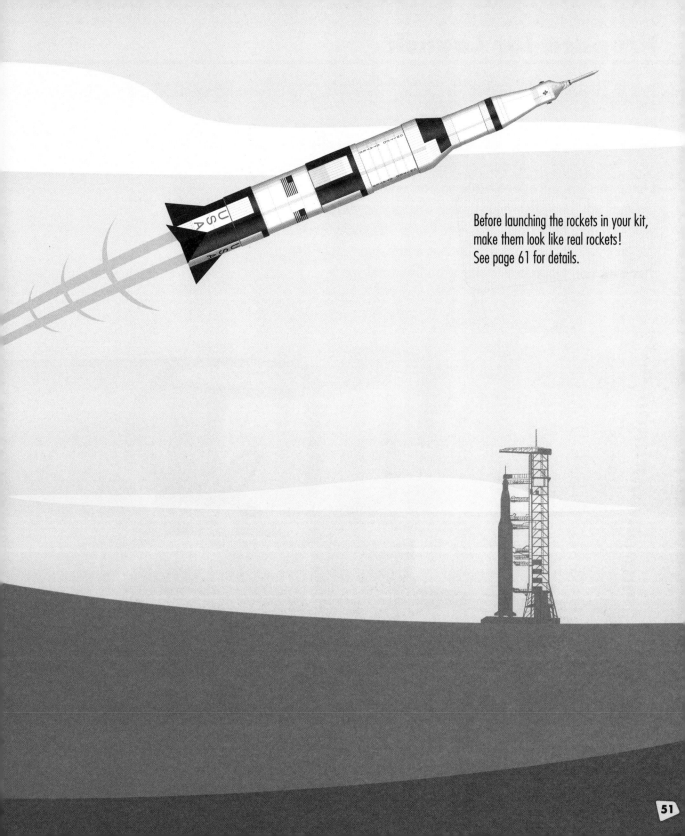

Before launching the rockets in your kit, make them look like real rockets! See page 61 for details.

Prepare for Launch

The first step in launching your rockets is choosing a launch site. Pick an open area where your rockets won't get stuck in trees, land on roofs, or hit power lines. Stay back from streets—you don't want your rockets falling onto cars when they land. You should steer clear of lakes, ponds, and streams, too. Otherwise you might end up taking an unexpected swim.

Once you have chosen a launch site, gather the materials you will need for launch. The only things you really need are the components from this kit. But there are some other things that might be fun to have, which are listed below:

Things to have for launch

A stopwatch to time flights

Tape measure (to measure distance from the launch pad)

Pencil and paper to log flights

Binoculars

Camera

A friend

CODE OF SAFETY · MODEL ROCKETRY

Model rocketeers follow a strict safety code.
The following parts of the code apply to the rockets in this kit.

▲ I will not launch my model rockets in high winds; near buildings, power lines, or tall trees; or under any conditions that might be dangerous to people or property.

▲ My model rockets will always be launched from a cleared area.

▲ To prevent accidental eye injury, I will never place my head or body over the launch pad.

▲ I will never attempt to recover my rocket from power lines or other dangerous places.

Did You Know?

Self-powered rockets travel slowly at the moment of launch. They go faster and faster as they rise. The air-powered rockets in this kit are just the opposite. They travel quickly at the moment of launch and slow down as they rise. This happens because the rockets are not creating any thrust, so air pressure and gravity quickly slow them down.

Launch Your Rockets

Now you're ready to launch your rockets! Just follow these 12 easy steps.

1. Insert rocket holder into base.

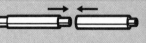

2. Insert the smaller end of tube 1 into tube 2.

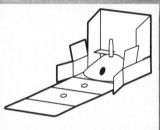

3. Insert the larger end of the connected tubes into the power source.

4. Fold up back of cardboard launch pad and fold in back flaps 1 and 2.

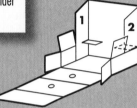

5. Fold tabs 1 and 2 to crease. Insert tab 1 into slot 1 and tab 2 into slot 2.

6. Insert rocket base into center of launch pad with the hole facing front.

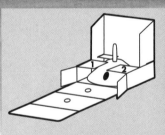

7. Fold side flaps 1 and 2 in toward the center of the launch pad.

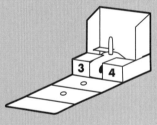

8. Fold side flaps 3 and 4 in toward the center of the launch pad.

9. Crease cover and cover tab on the lines. Lift cover straight up.

10. Slide the power source tube through the hole in the front of the cover and into the rocket base.

11. Fold cover in toward the back of the launch pad so that the rocket holder pokes through the hole in the top of the cover. Tuck the cover tab into the back of the launch pad.

12. Place the rocket onto the tube. Prepare for launch!

Angled Launch

The launcher is designed to shoot your rockets straight up. But you can launch your rockets at different angles by tilting the launch pad.

1. Set the launch pad and the attached air pump on a book. The book must be long enough to hold both items.

2. Slide more books or other sturdy items under the book's back edge to tilt the book. You can use a protractor to find the tile angle, or you can use the chart on this page as a reference.

3. Slide a rocket onto the launch stem.

4. Stand to the side, away from the rocket's launch path. Then push on the air pump.

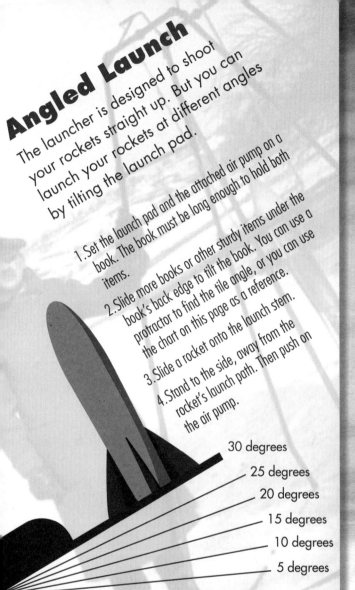

30 degrees
25 degrees
20 degrees
15 degrees
10 degrees
5 degrees

Be a Rocket Scientist!

You can experiment to see how different factors affect the flight of the rockets in this kit. The next few pages suggest a few things to try. But don't stop with the ideas in this book. Dream up your own experiments, then carry them out. The sky's the limit!

Real rocket scientists from the 1960s

Rocket Types

There are three different rockets in this kit:

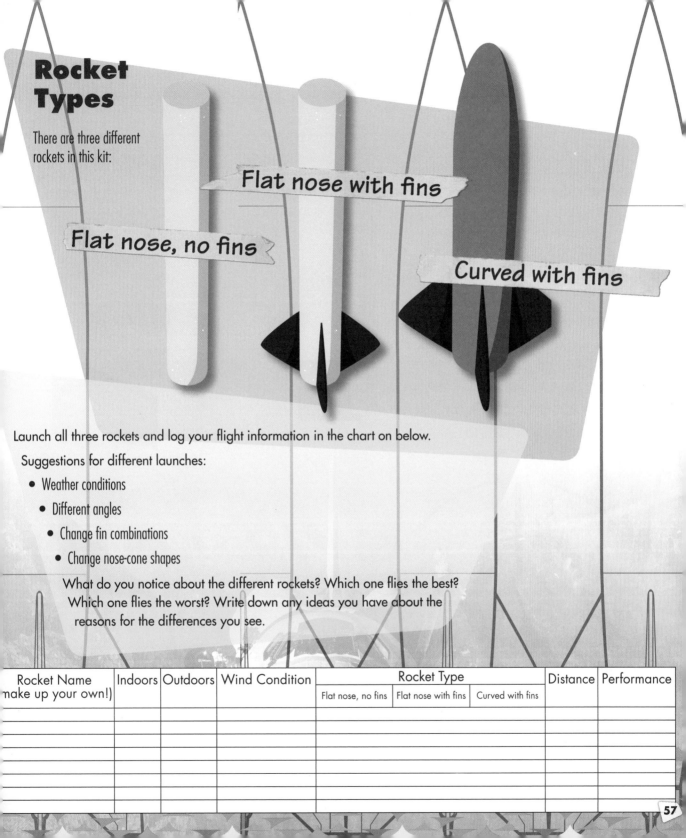

Flat nose with fins

Flat nose, no fins

Curved with fins

Launch all three rockets and log your flight information in the chart on below.

Suggestions for different launches:

- Weather conditions
- Different angles
- Change fin combinations
- Change nose-cone shapes

What do you notice about the different rockets? Which one flies the best? Which one flies the worst? Write down any ideas you have about the reasons for the differences you see.

Rocket Name (make up your own!)	Indoors	Outdoors	Wind Condition	Rocket Type			Distance	Performance
				Flat nose, no fins	Flat nose with fins	Curved with fins		

Fins

There are four basic rocket fin shapes:

Add each type of the fin to your "blank" rocket (flat nose, no fins) to see which shape works best. To add fins:

1. Make three copies of one of the shapes from this page on a piece of light cardboard, like an old file folder or an index card. Cut out the shapes.

2. Put a piece of masking tape along the inner edge of the shape.

3. Stick the shape to the rear end of your rocket.

4. Add another piece of masking tape on the other side of the shape to hold it in place.

5. Repeat Steps 2-4 with the other two shapes. Make sure the fins are spaced evenly around the rocket body.

Now you're ready to launch your rocket. How does it fly?

What happens if you use the other fin shapes?

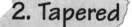

1. Elliptical

2. Tapered

3. Triangle

4. Rectangle

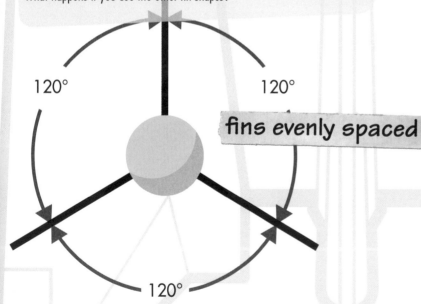

120°

120°

120°

fins evenly spaced

Nose Cones

Nose cones come in all shapes and sizes, depending on the design and function of the rocket. You can add different nose cones to the two flat-tipped rockets in this kit to see what difference they make.

Here are patterns for three different nose cones. Cone 1 has a radius of ½ inch (1.3cm); Cone 2 has a radius of 1 inch (2.5cm); Cone 3 has a radius of 1½ inches (3.8cm).

To make and attach a nose cone:

1. Trace any nose cone design from this page onto a piece of paper. Cut out the image.

2. Curl the paper into a cone. Tuck the flap underneath. Use a small piece of tape to hold the cone closed.

3. Use a thin strip of masking tape to attach the nose cone to the front end of your rocket.

Ready? It's launch time! Shoot your rocket into the air. Does it work differently than when it had a flat nose? What happens if you use the other two nose cone designs? Record your results and try to figure out the reasons for any differences you see.

½"
(1.3cm)

Cone 1

1"
(2.5 cm)

Cone 2

1 ½"
(3.8 cm)

Cone 3

What a Drag!
Nose cones are designed to reduce drag. A pointed nose cuts through the air more cleanly than a blunt nose.

Masking Tape

What happens if you:

• Attach the fins near the nose instead of the rear?

• Add four evenly spaced fins instead of three?

• Tape the fins on at a tilted angle?

• Bend the fins?

Did You Know?

Space rockets often carry their payloads in their noses. So the shape of a rocket's nose cone may depend on what the rocket needs to carry.

What's next?

The technology of rocket science has come a long way since its humble beginnings. From the earliest gunpowder rockets used for fireworks, to today's guided missiles that can find their target with amazing accuracy, rockets have evolved to serve many different purposes. They help to put satellites into orbit, which relay weather and other information. Astronauts rely on rockets to send them skyward so that space exploration can continue. And the military uses high-tech rockets as part of the country's defense program.

Although there have been many developments in the field of rocket science, one thing has remained constant: the desire to explore and improve the way the world works. Who knows what new discoveries lay ahead!

Make your rocket ... a rocket.

Just cut out the rocket "skin" along the black line with scissors, cut and fold the bottom where indicated to make the fins, wrap around the flat nose rocket (the one without fins), tape in place, and launch! (See page 54 for launching instructions.)

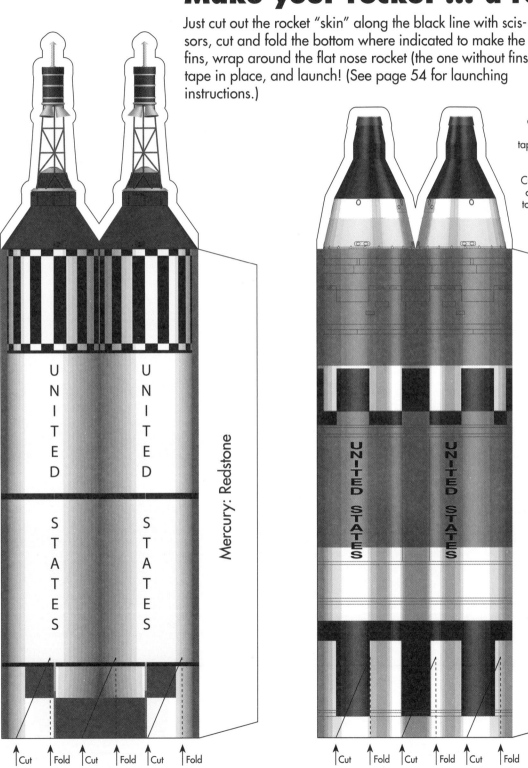

Mercury: Redstone

↑Cut ↑Fold ↑Cut ↑Fold ↑Cut ↑Fold

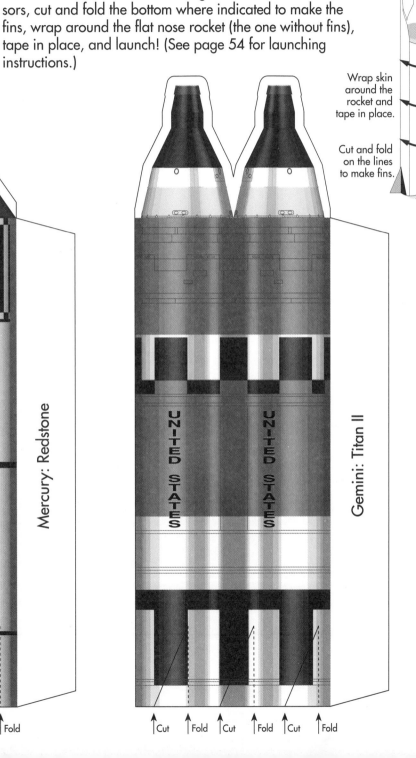

Wrap skin around the rocket and tape in place.

Cut and fold on the lines to make fins.

Gemini: Titan II

↑Cut ↑Fold ↑Cut ↑Fold ↑Cut ↑Fold

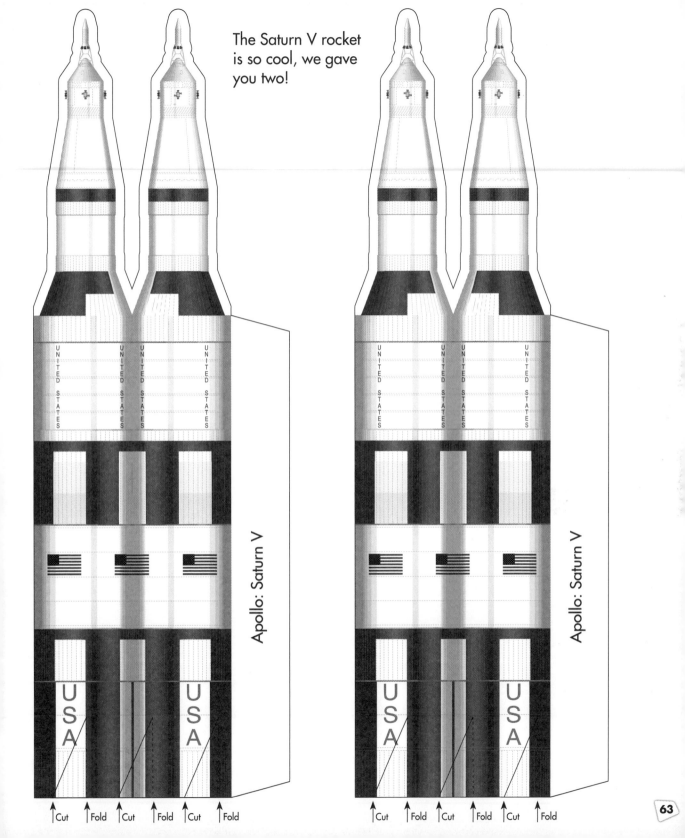

The Saturn V rocket is so cool, we gave you two!

Apollo: Saturn V

Apollo: Saturn V

UNITED STATES

USA

USA

USA

USA

↑Cut ↑Fold ↑Cut ↑Fold ↑Cut ↑Fold

↑Cut ↑Fold ↑Cut ↑Fold ↑Cut ↑Fold